THERE'LL BE A SLIGHT DELAY

THERE'LL BE A SLIGHT DELAY

And Other Poems for Grown-ups

Jack Prelutsky

Illustrations by Jack Ziegler

WILLIAM MORROW AND COMPANY, INC.
NEW YORK

Library of Congress Cataloging-in-Publication Data

Prelutsky, Jack.
    There'll be a slight delay : and other poems for grown-ups / Jack Prelutsky.
        p.   cm.
    ISBN 0-688-10791-5
    I. Title.
    PS3566.R36T47   1991
    811'.54—dc20   91-16025 CIP

Printed in the United States of America

First Edition

1 2 3 4 5 6 7 8 9 10

BOOK DESIGN BY DEBBIE GLASSERMAN

To Carolynn,
the woman who
is my beloved
POSSLQ

A 90'S TYPE GUY

Should I be macho?
Should I be mellow?
Spit on the sidewalk,
Or take up the cello?
Sip fine bottled water,
Or guzzle cheap beer?
It puzzles me, now that
The 90's are here.

I'm not at all certain
Just how to behave,
To help with the dishes,
Not bother to shave,
To belch at a ball game,
Attend the ballet.
Just what is expected
of menfolk today?

Should I be sensitive?
Should I be coarse?
Share my emotions,
Or fart like a horse?
Can anyone help me?
I'm anxious that I
Become an appropriate
90's type guy.

MY AMIGO MACK

Presenting my amigo Mack,
A chronic hypochondriac
Who unremittingly complains
About his nonexistent pains.
He says, as solemn as a Druid,
"I'm retaining too much fluid,
My malaises are severe,
I'll not live another year.

"Each of my extremities
Has got a different rare disease.
My lungs? I've little use for them,
They mostly manufacture phlegm.
My alimentary canal
Is undermining my morale,
A constant pounding wracks my chest,
I give myself a month at best.

"I hear a creaking in my bones,
And surely I have kidney stones,
Herpes, hives, and hepatitis,
German measles, gingivitis.
I get dizzy, qualmy, queasy,
Anxious, nauseous, and uneasy,
See the tic in my left cheek,
I'll be buried in a week.

"Look at me, my gums are bleeding,
And my hairline is receding,
Both my knees are stiff and swollen,
Something's stuck inside my colon.
I have hookworm, welts, and whiplash,
Blisters, cankers, and a lip rash,
Surely I am sinking fast,
Guess this day will be my last.

"Life is not a primrose garden,
Now my major vessels harden,
I could use a shot of plasma,
And I think I'm getting asthma.
I believe I have edema,
Hypertension, emphysema,
Jaundice, fever, and a chill,
I had best make out my will.

"I feel faint, my vision's blurry,
Ears are ringing, tongue is furry.
Respiration? Inconsistent.
Heartbeat? Almost nonexistent."
My amigo Mack is certain
They'll soon draw the final curtain,
So he's taken to his bed . . .
He survives—his doctor's dead.

SHE HAD NO PLACE TO SLEEP THAT NIGHT

She had no place to sleep that night,
He offered her his bed.
"I do it out of friendship!"
She nodded her sweet head.

"Platonic, yes!" they both agreed,
And eased beneath the covers.
They made their vow as midnight struck—
By morning, they were lovers.

I SAW A HOLY IMAGE IN A BOWL OF CHICKEN SOUP

I saw a holy image in a bowl of chicken soup
As I'd barely just begun my midday meal.
I notified the neighbors and a local Boy Scout troop,
They all verified that what I'd seen was real.

The golden yellow noodles were majestically arranged
Into something that transmogrified my soul.
Ever since that wondrous moment, my entire life has changed,
I'm the keeper of the famous holy bowl.

People stream into my kitchen for a glimpse of the divine,
And they never go away dissatisfied.
That image has transformed my simple home into a shrine,
And the noodles now are permanently dried.

"It's a sacred revelation!" "It's a symbol from above!"
"It's a miracle!" the pilgrims all agree.
I greet each sweet believer with humility and love,
And I only ask a very modest fee.

SHE'S LENA DEAN

She's Lena Dean, the "Condo Queen,"
Her eyes are blue, her money's green,
Her hubby made a ton of pelf,
And now she keeps it for herself.
She's overbearing, overdressed,
Impossible to not detest,
A self-important, pampered snob
Who dines on caviar and squab.

She's Lena Dean, the "Condo Queen,"
She's vitriolic, vain, and mean,
She spends, and then ignores her bills,
"I've got no time for them!" she trills.
She owns eleven Cadillacs,
And doesn't pay her income tax.
"Taxes? Ha!" she often jokes,
"They're only for the little folks."

"If I paid taxes"—Lena frowns—
How could I buy more velvet gowns,
More ruby rings, more sable coats,
More art nouveau, more planes, more boats,
More swimming pools, more priceless jade?
How could I keep my upstairs maid?"
Rapacious as a wolverine,
She's Lena Dean, the "Condo Queen."

TO A GENTLEMAN I DISLIKE

I give you, sir,
The time of day,
But just to speed you
On your way.

I'M WORRIED

I'm worried, as you might imagine,
For I've just begun to surmise
Spontaneous human combustion
Appears to be back on the rise.
Why only last weekend in Phoenix,
Two citizens burst into flames,
I recently read all about it,
The newspaper printed their names.

It surely was not their intention
To turn into smoldering pyres,
No doubt they were both discommoded
To note they were four-alarm fires.
It must be a trifle unnerving
To sense that your body's ablaze,
And likely the kind of condition
That bothers a fellow for days.

It often afflicts the pubescent,
And might be related to glands,
Whatever the reason, it's certain
To put a small crimp in their plans.
Perhaps it's their raging emotions
That rapidly turn them to ash,
In any event, it's apparent
That teenagers burn in a flash.

Still, most of the victims are older,
And somewhat removed from their prime,
Spontaneous human combustion
Can strike anyone anytime.
A friend telephoned me this morning,
I sensed his distress as he spoke,
"A sheriff not far from Sheboygan
Has suddenly gone up in smoke!"

My regular program this evening
Was cut unexpectedly short,
Preempted without prior warning
To air a disturbing report.
The newscaster said that in Tulsa,
A group had begun to ignite,
They seemed to be quite overheated,
And gave off a great deal of light.

When people start turning to cinders,
Their calorie counts tend to rise,
They often complain of a fever,
As temperatures climb to new highs.
I'm sure I'd be somewhat disheartened
When, sitting outside my porch,
I saw a pedestrian sizzle
And start to flare up like a torch.

It's made me a tad apprehensive,
Unable to tell who to trust.
I tend to steer clear of the neighbors,
In case *they* should start to combust.
This rash of abrupt conflagrations
Has got me increasingly vexed,
I'm keeping the garden hose handy,
In case *I* should incandesce next.

ON SCENT

It's time, I think, to pick a bone
With men who favor cheap cologne,
Especially the awful sorts
Available in pints and quarts,
(On special at the five-and-dime)
Which they apply to cheeks and necks
Like members of the fairer sex.

Their scents, so heavily applied,
Could drive a skunk to suicide,
Might frighten off a herd of yaks,
Or stop a tiger in its tracks.
They are my aromatic foes,
Those louts who sting my eyes and nose.
It simply is beyond my ken
Why they can't smell like decent men.

MY SWEET BELOVED POSSLQ

I wonder what on earth I'd ever do
Without my sweet beloved POSSLQ
   To make me feel I've blundered, and had better make amends,
   To constantly remind me that she doesn't like my friends,
   To mention that her mother never thought I was a prize,
   To laugh at my collection of suspenders, shirts, and ties,
   To castigate me daily with exotic bursts of prose,
   To single out, triumphantly, the pimple on my nose,
   To tell me every tale I tell's a tale I've told before,
   To comment that she knows I'm not a young man anymore,
   To mourn that my erotic skills have recently declined,
   To cite the excess baggage on my belly and behind,
   To chuckle that the hair atop my head is growing sparse,
   To snicker that I do not know my elbow from my arse,
   To indicate it's time to trim the fuzz upon my ears,
   To gloat that I'm discounted by my colleagues and my peers,
   To signal it's apparent that I never learned to drive,
   To quip, that by my diet, it's a wonder I'm alive,
   To notice every evening I could use another shave,
   To warn me I'm propelling her into an early grave,
   To regularly find new ways to put me in my place,
   To manage it with such aplomb, authority, and grace,
That I can only wonder what I'd do
Without my sweet beloved POSSLQ.

MONDAY WAS MONOTONOUS

Monday was monotonous,
Essentially a bore.
Tuesday was identical,
Perhaps a trifle more.
Wednesday was pathetic,
Not a single thing occurred.
Thursday turned out tedious,
Undoubtedly you've heard.

Friday was unvarying,
A day devoid of fun.
Saturday was colorless,
I slept from sun to sun.
Sunday was redundant,
Uneventful, pointless, dead.
I can't wait until tomorrow
Just to see what lies ahead.

THE DREADED HEMORRHOID

Worse than being unemployed
Is the dreaded hemorrhoid.
What a cruel trick of nature
To be a Preparation H'r!

THEIR BELOVED, TRUSTED GURU

Their beloved, trusted guru
Had charisma and panache,
They gave him their devotion,
Their possessions, and their cash.
He provided them a system
Of denial and delight,
He gave them each a mantra
Which they chanted day and night.

capistrano cuppa joe
crocka kaka calico
double dribble déjà vu
ishkabibble barbecue

Water was his sole libation,
He ate beans and nothing more,
They could tell that he was coming
Long before he reached their door.
So they bathed his blessed body
With exotic rare perfumes,
They obediently oiled him,
And they cleared his path with brooms.

jambalaya jericho
oleander oleo
inka dinka stinkaroo
bubble babble babalu

He was caring, he was giving,
He appeared to have no flaw,
He kept small and humble quarters,
Where he slept on lowly straw.
He wore nothing but a loincloth,
They put flowers in his hair,
He encouraged all their women
To discard their underwear.

noodle doodle daddy-o
sucker pucker piccolo
aura flora flopperoo
steala feely peekaboo

He had prepossessing whiskers,
Deep, intense, hypnotic eyes,
He could answer all their questions,
For though simple, he was wise.
He disseminated lessons
That would last them all their lives,
While they pondered his instruction,
He attended to their wives.

bull baloney bungalow
gaga raga romeo
cockamamie cockatoo
boola boola boogaloo

Then one morning they discovered,
To their horror and chagrin,
Their beloved, trusted guru
Had completely done them in.
For he took a sudden powder,
And made off with all the loot,
Leaving nothing but his mantra,
For he took their wives to boot.

goody goody gotta go
presto pianissimo
nooky whoopee royal screw
lamborghini iou

ON AN "ACTRESS"

She's loved by the public,
Adored by the press.
She fills a bikini,
Transfigures a dress.
She's garnered awards
From the Cinemacademy.
Her acting's indifferent,
But wow, what anatomy!

ON THOUGHTLESSNESS

Whenever I attend the nabes,
Some brainless broad with braying babes
Relaxes in a nearby seat
And lets her wretched infants bleat.
Oblivious to all around
Who have no wish to hear such sound,
She gives them leave to vent their spleen,
Distracting others from the screen.

The movie that I came to see,
The one for which I paid my fee,
Is ruined by these screaming brats
Who carry on like angry cats.
Is she too dense to realize
That no one wants to hear their cries?
Why can't the ninny use her dome,
And leave her lowing larvae home?

COMPUTER, COMPUTER

Computer, computer,
You tyrannous tool,
Whenever I use you
I feel like a fool.
I fail to distinguish
Your RAM from your ROM,
You drive me insane,
Though I try to stay calm.

Computer, computer,
You keep me off guard,
Your keyboard confounds me,
Your disk is too hard,
Your logic eludes me,
Your software's too firm,
Your windows are painful,
Your mouse makes me squirm.

Computer, computer,
I don't understand
Your easiest printer
Or scanner command,
Your pixels are puzzles,
I'm scared by your screen,
Your menu's a menace,
Your modem's obscene.

Computer, computer,
I can't interface,
Your floppies offend me,
Your data is base,
Your fonts make me flinch,
And your ports make me pule,
Computer, computer,
You tyrannous tool.

A STAUNCH REPUBLOCRAT

I am a staunch Republocrat
Whose party's never wrong,
Our platform's unimpeachable,
Our policies are strong.
The Demicans are nasty knaves
Who don't know how to dress,
They're patently the reason
For our current fiscal mess.

We're true to our constituents
And never deal in lies,
Unlike the other party's hacks
Who thrive on compromise.
Their leader has the wisdom
Of a catatonic trout,
I wish there were a way that we
Could throw the beggars out.

We're upright, moral, honest,
We behave as people should,
Our only vested interest
Is our nation's greater good.
We always vote our conscience
As we know we ought to do,
I am a staunch Republocrat—
Now who the hell are you?

ON MIMES

I think that it should be a crime
For anyone to be a mime.
A mime's an unappealing sight,
His "art" is crude, his antics trite.
His mannerisms are effete,
He blocks my progress down the street,
Then plays his pointless, puerile jokes,
And never talks like normal folks.

He dresses like a piece of fruit.
Why can't he wear a decent suit?
Why can't he find some honest work,
And stop behaving like a jerk?
He "climbs" imaginary stairs,
"Big deal!" I think. "So what? Who cares?"
He "tugs" a nonexistent rope,
I fear the fool has little hope.

He's "trapped" inside a phantom cage,
The imbecile should act his age.
He "sniffs" a bloom, he "rings" a bell,
He's ready for a padded cell.
A mime, who's of no earthly use
Deserves our unabridged abuse.
If I ever I could spare the time,
I'd like to stop and slap a mime.

ON FIGURINES

I've never seen a Hummel
That I didn't want to pummel.

THE GLADDEST WORDS

The gladdest words of pen or tongue?
"My, you're hung!"
The saddest that have ever been?
"Is it in?"

THEY DID IT IN THE SHOWER

They did it in the shower
And they did it in the tub,
They did it at the office
And they did it at the club,
They did it in a snowbank
And they did it at the lodge,
They did it in a limo
And they did it in a Dodge.

They did it on a sidewalk
And they did it on the floor,
They did it in a garden
And they did it at the store,
They did it in the desert
And they did it by the sea,
They did it on a saddle
And they did it up a tree.

They did it under tables
And they did it over chairs,
They did it in a closet
And they did it on the stairs,
They did it in the cellar
And they did it in the shed,
But they never did it better
Than they did it in their bed.

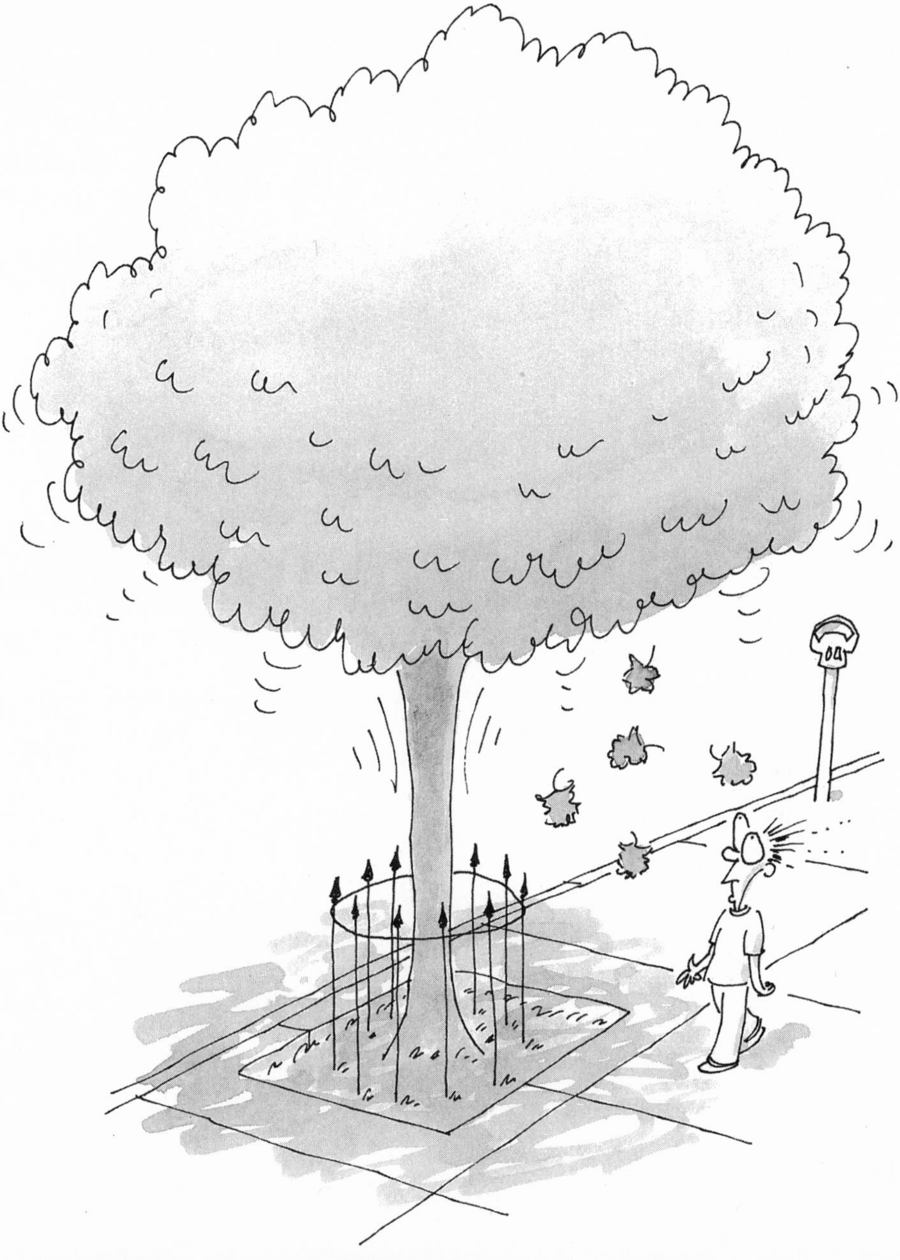

MY QUEST FOR IMMORTALITY

My quest for immortality
Will triumph, cryogenically.
Scant seconds after I am dead,
They'll lop off my distinguished head,
And stuff it in a strange device
Where it will slumber, safe on ice.
The rest they'll bury in some position
Selected by a trained mortician.

Though I will long have bought the farm,
My head won't suffer further harm,
But safe from famine and disease,
Remain intact for centuries.
At last some clever future folk
Will cure the blight that made me croak,
And when the ice is scraped away,
My head will see the light of day.

They'll bond it to a sturdy frame
That from then on will bear my name.
My new physique will be designed
To top the one I left behind.
I'll rise, I'll stretch, I'll smile, I'll wave,
Perhaps I'll visit my own grave.
I'll never sniffle, sneeze, or cough—
If the power fails, all bets are off!

ON CHEER

I'd like to strangle straightaway
The shnooks who say, "Have a nice day!"
And catapult to outer space,
The drones who draw the "happy face."

FAT OLD MAN ON ROLLERBLADES

Fat old man on Rollerblades,
Wearing shorts and sporting shades,
Frail of limb and false of tooth,
Searching for your vanished youth.

Can you thus relive your past,
Up on wheels and going fast?
Likely you'll run out of gas,
Or fall down and break your ass.

ODES ON AN ODIOUS ROOMMATE

I
Oh roommate mine, you'd not be missed
Had you remained a blastocyst.
And if today you meet your doom,
Tomorrow I shall rent your room.

II
Waking in the midst of day,
Staring in your coffee cup,
If you've nothing bad to say,
You will soon make something up.

III
You smoke revolting cigarettes,
Your clothes, unwashed, reek of your pets.
Your breath is rank, your odor bitter,
I call it "eau de kittilitter."

IV

Oh were you sweet butter,
You'd surely turn sour,
And were you a garden,
I'd sniff not a flower,
And were you bright metal,
You'd tarnish and rust,
And were you cold ashes,
I'd frequently dust.

V

When you do not haunt these rooms,
You're shopping for replacement brooms.

VI

Heart of bituminous,
Bite of a shark,
Were bitchiness luminous,
You'd glow in the dark.

VII

The rent is due,
But where are you?

VIII

Were you an alligator's child
These songs might not be sung,
For crocodilians, wise though wild,
At times consume their young.

A BOLD CANADIAN PIG

It was a bold Canadian pig
That fled the abattoir,
Escaping swiftly through a door
Left carelessly ajar.
The butchers bolted after him,
Their cleavers fast in hand,
But Francis (for that was his name)
Outran that bloody band.

The butchers combed the neighborhood,
It was to no avail,
For all they glimpsed of Francis
Was his little curly tail.
They trailed him up, they trailed him down,
He did not give a hoot,
That pig was too resourceful,
And eluded their pursuit.

They summoned skillful trackers,
But their efforts came to naught,
They tried their best to capture him,
That pig would not be caught.
The country's finest force was called,
He did not care a fig,
A Mountie always gets his man,
But often not his pig.

In every situation
Francis won the upper hand,
The legends of his escapades
Soon grew throughout the land.
That porker was a hero
That nobody could confine,
A living inspiration,
And the nation's finest swine.

Then winter came, and many feared
His life would soon be lost,
They hoped to bring him safe inside,
Removed from chill and frost.
A hunter was enlisted,
A courageous, bold Canuck,
But though he strived to save that pig,
That pig was out of luck.

The hunter had no wish to harm,
It was his sole intent
To tranquilize that worthy pig
Without that pig's consent.
He gamely dogged his quarry,
And through chance and fortitude,
He soon had Francis in his sights—
Alas! That pig was screwed.

A shot rang out, the pig was struck
Betwixt his head and thighs,
It caused a great infection,
And his premature demise.
Now Francis sleeps that final sleep
From which no pig may waken,
The missile failed to save his hide,
And fixed his Canadian bacon.

SHE WAS ONCE A YUPPIE PRINCESS

She was once a Yuppie Princess
Making lots of lovely cash,
She possessed a golden future,
Yet today she's slinging hash.
For the market plunged abruptly,
And she lost her Wall Street job,
Now she can't afford her condo,
And she's had to sell her Saab.

Her position was prestigious
In the world of high finance,
Now she's barely making ends meet,
And she rails at circumstance.
Her mobility is downward,
It's a common trend today,
She's another brilliant waitress
With a useless MBA.

CLASSIFIED AD

I cannot stand the sight of me,
I hate the way I talk,
My posture is preposterous,
I loathe the way I walk.
My features are repugnant,
And my clothing's often soiled,
My manners are atrocious,
And my hair is thickly oiled.

My breath is reprehensible,
I wear an ugly scowl,
My bodily effluvium
Is flatulently foul.
I haven't any energy,
My thinking's uninspired,
And what I've got inside my shorts
Leaves much to be desired.

I'm thoroughly unwholesome,
Like the content of my food,
And since I drink around the clock,
I'm generally stewed.
I'm always short of money,
And I've never held a job,
I'm undersexed and overweight,
An unremitting slob.

I'm searching for that soulmate
Who's been searching just for me,
If you're not too particular,
Then I'm your cup of tea.
Are you that special someone
I'm so anxious to adore?
Please call me soon at five-five-five—
Three-seven-seven-four.

ON DOO

I've now a spate of angry words
For those whose dogs deposit turds
On path and alley, street and stoop,
And then do not remove the poop.
I've not the slightest wish to step
In doody left by Spot or Shep
Or Rex or other wretched pup—
Why can't their owners pick it up?

I'd gladly take a leather strap
To those who let their canines crap
Upon a public thoroughfare
And blithely leave the droppings there.
Since they're more vulgar than their hounds,
Perhaps they should be housed in pounds,
Kept on a leash, or caged in zoos,
These fools whose mutts befoul my shoes.

I WATCHED A TELEVANGELIST

I watched a televangelist
Emoting on the screen.
His smile was uninviting,
Though his teeth were mighty clean.
His two-tone polyester suit
Had extra-wide lapels,
And he preached his pious message
With enthusiastic yells.

"HALLELUJAH! LET US PRAY!
OPEN UP YOUR PURSE TODAY!
GIVE ME ALL YOU CAN AFFORD!
PASS THE LOOT AND PRAISE THE LORD!"

A woman stood beside him
Clad in alabaster white.
She seemed a tad unearthly,
And not altogether bright.
Her coiffure was gold and silver,
I was startled by its size.
Her hands were clasped in rapture,
Teardrops welled within her eyes.

"HALLELUJAH! WRITE A CHECK!
IT WILL HELP YOU SAVE YOUR NECK!
NEVER EAT FORBIDDEN FRUIT!
PRAISE THE LORD AND PASS THE LOOT!"

He pounded on his Bible,
and he pointed at the sky.
He promised if we followed him,
We'd never truly die.
Her face was flushed with fervor,
Her pneumatic bosom heaved.
They were both so damn convincing
That I almost half believed.

      "HALLELUJAH! SEND IT IN!

      EVERY DOLLAR SHEDS A SIN!

      YOU WILL REAP A RICH REWARD!

      PRAISE THE LOOT AND PASS THE LORD!"

WE'D BEEN APART FOR MANY YEARS

We'd been apart for many years,
Then met one day by chance.
I hoped we might rekindle
The flame of our romance.

But we could neither touch nor speak,
The fates conspired to spite us,
For she had poison ivy,
and I had laryngitis.

ON ROAD HOGS

I do believe I'd like to brain
The snails who hog the passing lane,
And I would smite with great delight
The swine who pass me on the right.

UFOs ARE REALLY HERE

Every day, in our great nation,
There's a bovine mutilation,
Ruminants are being found
Disembowled on the ground.
From Secaucus to Seattle,
Something's cutting up our cattle,
And the explanation's clear—
UFOs are really here.

They're here! They're here! These UFOs,
And manned by alien so-and-sos
Who visit us with carving knives
To terminate our livestock's lives.
Herds of cattle, nicely fattened,
Suddenly are being flattened
And dismembered by battalions
Of these outer space rapscallions.

They have come across light-years
Just to disassemble steers,
Deputy sheriffs have reported
This behavior, strange and sordid.
Such unseemly vivisection
Spoils a healthy cow's complexion.
Go back to your own galaxy—
Or mutilate some broccoli!

ON GOLFERS

It's a snap to spot the golfers,
Even in the densest crowd.
Their demeanors will be quiet,
But their trousers will be loud.
They're invariably fellows,
You will notice at a glance,
With the odd predisposition
To affect outlandish pants.

The patterns are preposterous,
The taste grotesquely bad—
A wretched check, a lurid stripe,
An aggravating plaid.
They pick inane materials
To cover their behinds.
Their bottoms make me wonder
What goes on in golfers' minds.

YES, PERHAPS I'M BEING PICKY

Yes, perhaps I'm being picky,
And excessively absurd,
But I deeply feel that "aspic"
Is a coarse and vulgar word.

THERE'LL BE A SLIGHT DELAY

Our captain spoke laconically,
"There'll be a slight delay."
I knew from long experience
I'd not get home today.
He intimated trouble
With a small but vital part.
I could feel my stomach churning,
And a clutching at my heart.

Our stewardess was buoyant,
"We'll be airborne in a while."
I could sense her apprehension,
Irrespective of her smile.
A mechanic shortly entered,
Looking thoroughly displeased
As he grimly eyed the cockpit
Like he thought it was diseased.

Our captain next confided
In his reassuring drawl,
"We are working on the problem,
It should not take long at all.
We'll install a new component
Just as quickly as we can.
We expect it any moment,
It's on order from Japan."

Our stewardess advised us
In a voice controlled yet cute,
That according to her info,
We'd be presently en route.
But we sat there for an hour,
And another hour more,
Till my patience was exhausted,
And my bottom stiff and sore.

We all began to fidget,
And our mood was growing dark,
The boldest of us grumbled
That we'd like to disembark.
We were hungry, bored and tired,
But the crew was inhumane,
And despite our protestations
Wouldn't let us off the plane.

Our captain just admitted,
"Folks, it can't be fixed today.
We've got another flight for you
Just eighty gates away.
It departs in twenty minutes,
If you run with all your might,
I am reasonably confident
You still can make that flight.

"We regret the inconvenience,
But it's really not our fault.
It's a storm in the Pacific
That has brought us to a halt.
From everyone at Air Bizarre
We wish you all good-bye.
Please come back soon—and think of us
When next you need to fly.

ON YOUTH

I haven't got the least respect
For teenage boys who get erect.
A girl walks by, they think "romance!"
And there's a stirring in their pants.

They're often seated on the bus,
And though I do not make a fuss,
It bothers me to see them rise
In public, right before my eyes.

Some try to hide it with a coat,
But all the same, it gets my goat,
And, yes, I feel a quiet rage
That I can't match them at my age.

SONNETS

I

Unswervable, I'm firm upon this point:
I'll masticate no provender that's crude.
With this in mind, I'm blind to every joint
Which serves the pinguid swill yclept "fast food."
Fast food! Swift aliment bereft of soul,
Your stench offends my nose, your sight, my eyes.
You clog the pores, you raise cholesterol.
Begone, abhorrent burgers, ghastly fries!
I gag when gluttons stuff their guts with grease
Which, glob on glob, coagulates (adheres
To tortured innards), making them obese,
And prone to grim afflictions all their years.
    Sweet life's too brief to fill our frames with fat
    Unfit to feed the foulest filthy rat.

II

You couch potatoes, spuds of the divan,
Suspended in a soporific state,
Apparently, your only earthly plan
Is gleaning how you best may vegetate.
You loll about on sofas, slouch in chairs,
In postures both pathetic and obscene,
Your faces, frozen masks with glassy stares,
Transfixed by forms which flicker on a screen.
At times, commercial messages appear,
Then, magically, you waken from your thrall,
Perhaps to open yet another beer,
Perhaps to answer nature's urgent call.
    Returning, you resume your wretched role.
    Vicarious, you crave remote control.

III

I know of none who loves a meter maid,
That wench afoot who prowls the urban strand,
And plies her unessential, pointless trade
With packs of dread citations fast in hand.
She neither manufactures useful wares,
Nor furnishes some service humans need.
No motorist who drives the thoroughfares
Would mourn the swift extinction of her breed.
The flag begins to fall, she starts to write,
Her pencil notes your dire offense, your fine.
You're there! You plead. Her ears are sealed. Despite
Your epithets, she scribes another line.
    What jinn made my metropolis create
    A jade who only serves to irritate?

IV

My doctor speaks. "You've caught a rare disease!
It's fatal! There's no cure! You face your doom!"
I fall upon my knees. He says, "My fees
Are due in full before you leave this room!"
Days pass. I suffer tests. He speaks. "You're worse!
It's evident you've but a little while!
Perhaps you'd best engage a private nurse!
Now pay me—and let's see that winning smile!"
Weeks pass. My heart is filled with dark despair.
The phone!!! He speaks. "I've erred! You are not ill!"
Then drones, as I sit sobbing in my chair,
"This will, of course, be added to my bill!"
  I have my health. I'm penniless. He spends
  My savings on a rare Mercedes-Benz.

V

At dawn, my neighbor, deep in winter's years,
Dives headlong in the surf to swim a race,
And thrashing there, amidst a sea of peers,
Disdainful of his pain, maintains his pace.
When, gasping, he at last alights ashore,
He mounts a frail but swift velocipede,
Then pedals for a hundred miles and more,
To further test endurance, pluck and speed.
You'd think he'd have enough by now, but no!
There yet remains a distance to be run.
With breathing labored, steps both short and slow,
His ancient frame performs a marathon.
    He finishes at nightfall, near collapse.
    Why can't he act his age and take long naps?

VI

I know a man, inept and insecure,
A timid wimp, milk-livered all his life.
His will is weak, his self-esteem is poor,
He's daunted by his children, fears his wife.
From time to time he gets behind the wheel,
And then (and only then!) he finds his spine.
No longer is he but a poor shlemiel,
His jaw is firm, his heart is leonine.
He glowers at pedestrians with scorn,
Accelerates through every yellow light.
He weaves through traffic, leaning on the horn,
Then flips a bird, and passes on the right.
   Inherently, he seems to understand
   The power of vehicular command.

VII

"We welcome you aboard our friendly flight.
Our captain swears we'll soon be under way.
You'd better make those seat belts extra tight.
The turbulence is moderate today.
We're proud to serve you peanuts for your lunch.
Refrain from flushing objects down the drain.
Locate the nearest exits. I've a hunch
They're dandy if we need to flee the plane.
And if the cabin should depressurize,
Forget you're nearly petrified to death.
A mask will fall. We've one convenient size.
Affix it. Stop your screaming. Take a breath.
   Get comfy now. You're safe on Air Elite.
   Flotation aids are stowed beneath your seat."

VIII

I've met some men, a cut above the rest,
Impeccable, imbued with savoir faire.
Their suits (from Savile Row) are neatly pressed,
They choose the perfect shirts and ties to wear.
They keep a flawless polish on their shoes,
They're certain of the seemly thing to say,
They even know the proper fork to use.
They are . . . how shall I put it? Distingué!
They find the most befitting gifts to give,
They radiate self-confidence and charm,
They recognize precisely how to live,
Their postures are correct, their smiles are warm.
    They're virtuous, felicitous, refined.
    A pox on them! We do not need their kind.

IX

Two costumed whoppers, sweating by the quart,
Great beefy bumpkins, thick of wit and thews,
Are met to grapple in that pseudo-sport
Which operates on predetermined cues.
Each swaggers like some savage, pagan king
As they commence to consummate their fraud.
They toss each other hard about the ring,
As hordes of unwashed citizens applaud.
"The Masked Malfeasor" falls, no longer game,
He's counted out, and feigns a broken bone.
"The Brazen Bane" again sustains his claim
Of higher levels of testosterone.
   What drives these louts to train in rancid gyms
   To learn how best to twist another's limbs?

X

"Our bellman's rather busy!" sniffed the clerk,
An unimpressive ass with pompous airs.
The ancient elevator didn't work,
I labored up eleven flights of stairs.
My room was stale, one dingy fixture shone,
The mattress sagged, I stepped on dusty rugs.
The plumbing leaked, and I was not alone . . .
I numbered nine varieties of bugs.
The window wouldn't budge. The walls (too thin!)
Admitted sounds too ardent to ignore.
Exhausted, I elected to dine in.
I ordered lunch at one, it came at four.
    The food was cold, the fool forgot the fork.
    I always stay here when I'm in New York.

XI

The fairest of all maids assembled there
Approaches with a smile. I think, "She's mine!"
I happily inhale her fragrant hair,
And then she blithely chirrups, "What's your sign?"
My features fall, I sigh, my brain goes blank.
Her question is sincere, she does not jest.
I know her now as just another crank,
Although I yet admire her ample breast.
She studies me with bright, inviting eyes,
"I'm Taurus!" I believe I hear her say.
"Beware of Dog!" I bark. (Did I disguise
My sentiments?) She blanches, breaks away.
   How many days have there been words I've said
   Which cost me nights of ecstasy in bed?

XII

I am a man not meant to mow a lawn,
That tragic thatch of tough, entangled greens.
If I've a need to demonstrate my brawn,
I'll wrestle, or enlist in the Marines.
I'd sooner stuff an onion up my nose,
Let clumsy doctors irrigate my ears,
Than have to spend a moment more with those
Infernal tools, the mower, rake, and shears.
On Sunday I, unconscious in the house,
Avoiding any labor that I can,
Am wakened by a sermon from my spouse,
"The grass is high—go mow it like a man!"
    Why can't we hire a large and limber child,
    Or simply let the stinking stuff grow wild?

XIII

Unhappy ostentatious billionaire
Whose puss is often plastered in the press,
You've managed to amass a lion's share
Of symbols of American success.
You blatantly confess you're pressed for pelf,
You're strapped for bucks, your back's against the wall.
I'm thunderstruck! I'm quite beside myself
Just thinking of your shrinking wherewithal.
I fear you'll have to sail a smaller yacht.
Champagne? Alack, you'll quaff a lesser brand.
Bid caviar adieu, poor plutocrat,
No doubt you'll soon be begging, hat in hand.
   I hear you now . . . "I've fallen on hard times.
   Say, brother, can you spare a billion dimes?"

XIV

I'm sitting in a dismal luncheonette,
Considering how best to fill my hide.
The specialty today is fish croquette
With peas and mashed potatoes on the side.
The menu lists a venomous array
Of edibles unworthy of the name.
The nearest town is twenty miles away,
Reputedly, the food is much the same.
Though famished, I've not nerve enough to try
The chicken wings, cheese fingers, or their ilk.
I settle on a slab of soggy pie,
And wash it down with slightly soapy milk.
   Comestibles one cannot quite digest
   Are plentiful throughout our great Midwest.

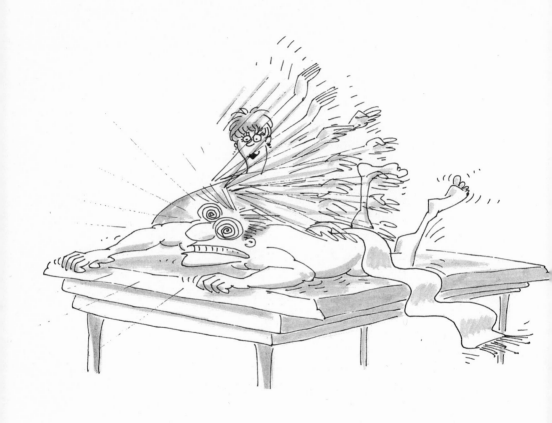

XV

I'm naked, prone, and helpless on a bench,
She smears me with an evil-smelling oil.
Unmindful of the stench, she starts to wrench
My shoulders from my neck as I recoil.
She twists a thigh, assails an upper arm,
She stretches things you'd never think could stretch.
I cry out in discomfort and alarm.
"Chill out!" she chides. "Relax! Don't be a kvetch!"
She kneads me like a yeasty lump of dough.
Her vigor grows, I cannot take much more.
My shrieks become a shrill fortissimo,
As muscles ache which never ached before.
   Once weekly I submit to this abuse.
   She is, of course, my favorite masseuse.

XVI

The papers say that crime is on the rise,
There's been a major oil spill off the coast,
A trusted politician's telling lies,
A psycho socked a noted talk show host,
Our government is deeper in the red,
A beauty queen was eaten by a shark,
A jogger found another severed head,
Tornadoes have destroyed a trailer park,
A hunter accidentally shot his friend,
Recidivists are out on work release,
As acid rain continues to descend,
And millions are egregiously obese.
    My heart is light, my sentiments sublime,
    My team has won in triple overtime.

XVII

Habitués of dim "adult arcades,"
Salacious in your every waking thought,
How furtively you ogle undraped maids
In sleazy magazines you haven't bought.
You slaver over breast and gaping crotch,
You drool as you unfold each double spread,
The movies you assiduously watch
Would make a gynecologist turn red.
You skulk in seedy theaters day on day,
Where every film is rated "Triple X,"
Excited by the unabashed display
Of monumental cinematic sex.
    You thrive on strangers' deeds between the sheets,
    I will say this—it keeps you off the streets.

XVIII

The shoppers at "The Sleek Unique Boutique,"
Which smugly caters to the "upper end,"
Are swarming in an open-credit clique,
To passionately spend and spend and spend.
They wear the most contemporary clothes,
And only in sophisticated hues,
Designer jeans, distinctly patterned hose,
Expensive silken scarves, imported shoes.
These ladies, all unconscionably rich,
From debutante to venerable dame,
Refuse to don a solitary stitch,
Unless it bears its famous maker's name.
    Shall I compare them to a herd of steers,
    These broads with brands emblazoned on their rears?

XIX

I've never heard the language that he speaks,
He chatters, notwithstanding his catarrh,
His hair's unkempt, his body oddly reeks,
And air is thick within the yellow car.
He gestures that he knows the way to go,
I sense he is a less than honest man,
We race away, yet my suspicions grow,
He seems to drive by way of Pakistan.
We turn a corner previously turned,
I remonstrate, he flashes me a grin.
We're there at last, and clearly I've been burned,
The fare is triple what it should have been.
   I tip him well, unwilling to complain—
   How grand to get a taxi in the rain!

XX

I know a woman desperate for love,
Who swears she'll cherish anyone in pants.
She doesn't care if he's a hawk or dove,
Disheveled, deaf and dumb, or cannot dance.
She wants a man who's macho or a wimp,
She'll take him though he hasn't bathed all year,
She needs him if he's childish as a chimp,
Unstable, or as stupid as a steer.
The man she seeks is either old or young,
He's short or tall, his head may have no hair.
She says he doesn't have to be well-hung,
As long as there's a little something there.
    She'll love him if he's human, more or less,
    Unless, of course, he's with the IRS.

XXI

I'm fifty now, and longer in the tooth,
My locks, once raven black, are leaden gray.
Though in my heart I'm still a slender youth,
Apparently, I'm not perceived that way.
Now every ounce of aliment I eat,
Bran, barley, bacon, berry, bean, or Brie,
Goes quickly to my center and my seat,
Becoming yet another ounce of me.
I suffer in additional respects
Which pain me more than my increasing spread,
I find instead of craving frequent sex,
I'm satisfied to simply read in bed.
    And finally, what makes my senses numb
    Is knowing that the worst is yet to come.